Have you ever thought about the possibility of using single words to spark ideas about managing well, both in the business world and in your personal lives? *300 Dictums* lists and defines verbs that describe actions, which can provoke results. Use *300 Dictums* to help inspire some of your own thoughts that will make you more effective in managing your business as well as your life.

KUDOS for *300 Dictums*

300 Dictums by J. Robert Parkinson is a fascinating book. He gives action verbs a whole new meaning by making them motivational and inspirational. It's impossible, at least for me to rate the book, as I don't think there are any other books even close to it to compare it to. So let me just say that whether you are writing, or simply looking for inspiration and motivation to improve your life, this is a very handy book to have. You'll want to keep it close and refer to it often. ~ *Taylor Jones, Reviewer*

300 Dictums by J. Robert Parkinson is a reference book of the first order. The premise of the book is to spark ideas using action verbs or action words and listing their inspirational and motivational definitions. This handy reference guide is a must for authors, speech writers, or anyone who wants or needs to use words that will inspire and motivate themselves and others, making them more effective in both their business and personal communications. The book is jam-packed ideas to help you get the most out of your language. As reference books go, this one is on the top of the heap. ~ *Regan Murphy, Reviewer*

ACKNOWLEDGEMENTS

Although they don't realize it, many people have contributed to this book.

Over the years I have read and heard the comments contained in these pages, and I have been the "collector" rather than the "creator" of the thoughts.

I can't name them all, but I want to acknowledge them for their wisdom, their sensitivity, and their willingness to help colleagues, friends, family, and total strangers to use their time and talents well, both personally and professionally.

Thank you all for what you have done for all of us for so long.

300 DICTUMS

Or, as Caesar would say: *CCC DICTA*.
(Direct your life, your job, your day
~ one verb at a time.)

J. Robert Parkinson, Ph.D.

A Black Opal Books Publication

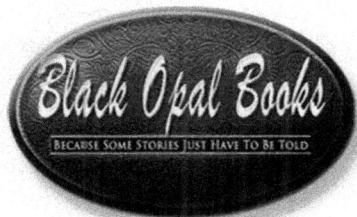

Black Opal Books
BECAUSE SOME STORIES JUST HAVE TO BE TOLD

GENRE: NON-FICTION/MOTIVATIONAL/INSPIRATIONAL/SELF-
HELP

300 DICTUMS
© 2014 by J. Robert Parkinson
All Rights Reserved
Cover Design by J. Robert Parkinson
© 2014 All Rights Reserved
Print ISBN: 978-1-626942-05-9

First publication: JANUARY 2015

Published by Black Opal Books: **http://www.blackopalbooks.com**

DEDICATION

To my wife, Eileen
Always an inspiration,
And always my
First Editor

INTRODUCTION

A few years ago, I coauthored a book titled, *Becoming a Successful Manager*. As the name suggests it focused on suggestions and techniques newly appointed managers can use to carry out their new responsibilities. The book includes a wide variety of anecdotes, stories, and exercises to provide guidance and to avoid problems with a new job.

Then I authored another book titled, *Mottoes for Managing* in which I used "one-liners" to serve as thinking points for effective managing. Next I thought about the possibility of using single words to spark ideas about managing well – managing both in the business world and in personal lives.

This book, *300 Dictums*, is the result. Every one of

the three hundred entries is deliberately short – only a few sentences.

My intent is to suggest the action, then to give a brief "jump-start" to thinking about the implications of the action verb.

I went for an economy of words because a single word can evoke multiple thoughts. I selected "verbs" rather than other parts of speech because verbs describe actions, and actions provoke results, which have consequences.

Why three hundred items? It seemed to be a good compromise. When I started writing this book, I considered doing 365 entries – one for every day if the year.

Seemed reasonable.

But since the verbs are focused primarily on work-related activities, and we all know that no one works every day of the year, I calculated actual workdays per year.

Counting holidays and vacations, that came to about 200 days.

So I looked for a nice round number between the 200 workdays and the 365 total days. Three hundred seemed to make sense, so that's what I picked.

That's as good a reason as any I can think of, and I hope the verbs I have selected will provoke some of your own thoughts.

That will expand the ultimate impact of this book.

I hope you find these thoughts interesting and valuable. Let me know what you think. I'd like to hear from you.

Please e-mail me at: jrp@jrparkinson.com.

HOW TO READ THIS
BOOK – OR NOT!!

Most people start to read a book just the way you did – at the beginning. That makes good sense because you have to start somewhere, and it's logical to flip open the front cover and begin. But now I'd like to suggest something different. These verbs are arranged in alphabetical order, but that was only so I'd be able to avoid duplication. I had to know what verbs were already included as I worked thought the entire text. All the letters of the alphabet are not equally represented – in fact some are missing entirely.

But, don't read them in alphabetical order!

Don't just turn page after page and then read left to right, top to bottom. That works for most books because a planned sequence is necessary in many books. Not this one.

You decide the order. Be random.

This book is designed to be an exploration of ideas, and like all explorations, pick the route that seems to make the most sense to you. Move from idea to idea, unconstrained by typical book-reading conventions. Jump around. As you skip from page to page and idea to idea, you'll discover some similarities from item to item. That's not only okay, but also it's important to realize these similarities in business and family life.

No two items are exactly alike, just as no two situations at home or on the job are exactly alike. To help you hop, skip, and jump through the book, and to help you overcome the old habit of reading from page one to the end, I'd like to suggest something for fun as well as for discipline.

Don't, under any circumstances or for any reason, read the page following this section. When you finish this brief section, flip to somewhere in the middle of the book. When you find that page, don't read the top item. Read something else.

This might seem a little strange – and perhaps a little silly – but I'd like you to grab on to an idea and then just think about it for a while. Consider how the idea might affect your life and your work. The entries are deliberately short, so you can scan them quickly and then add your own ideas. There is plenty of space for you to write your own thoughts.

I hope my ideas and suggestions will spark some of yours. Let that spark ignite and burn. Both light and heat will be the result of this exercise.

As you work your way through the book in this manner, you might revisit an item you have already read. That, too, is okay because reading it a second or third time could produce a different idea in your mind – a different spark and a different flame.

So let's give it a try. Turn to a page somewhere well into the book. Don't read the top item, read something else. Then read subsequent pages in whatever sequence you select.

But remember – for fun and for the discipline – don't read the next page.

It has absolutely nothing to do with the rest of this book. When you have read all three hundred items, go to the last page for a final wrap up.

Now move into the book – and enjoy.

WHY ARE YOU
READING THIS PAGE?

S ee what habits can do? You're so used to turning page after page, you did it here, even though I told you not to do that.

There is nothing of significance on this page.

Now try again. Move well into the book. Select a page. Don't read the top item.

After that, you're on your own. Feel free to read any page in any order – but please don't turn to this page again.

Have fun.

ACCEPT the idea that your subordinates have good ideas too. As managers, you're not endowed with omniscience. Collaborate with others to identify the best possible ideas, solutions, and courses of action

ADDRESS all opportunities and problems as soon as they are identified. If you ignore them, they won't go away, and they usually won't fix themselves either. Take action and take charge. Take the initiative

ADVANCE as many ideas and proposals as you receive after you have reviewed them. Also, comment on their value and appropriateness. Keep information flowing in three directions – up, down, and laterally. Keep everyone informed, all the time.

ADVERTISE your ideas, your interests, and your expectations. Advertising doesn't happen only in the media. It happens in and with everything you do and say to those around you. Be sure that your total message is clear to those around you. Use all the tools you have available.

AGREE to disagree. This is often said, but equally often ignored. By making this clear to those around you, you demonstrate you value their ideas, and you respect their positions. In the end, you might not follow their suggestions, but that's okay. They will know they had an opportunity to participate.

AIM for the clearest target. Determine what you want to accomplish. What and who do you need? What time frame is appropriate? Without a clear target your efforts might be misdirected, and your efforts wasted.

ALLOW others to have their say. They might just come up with ideas you never considered. Be sure you make it easy – and safe – for others to express themselves concerning the business, the department, the company, or the family. Benefit from the total talent available.

ANNOUNCE your decisions as soon as you make them. Also, advise others when you are pondering a decision. Keep them informed about your intentions. You don't have to provide all the details, but let others know you are "working on it."

ANSWER questions as soon as they are asked. If you don't have sufficient information to provide a complete answer, let others know what you're up to. Don't leave information gaps, or others will fill those gaps with their own expectations. That could cause you even more problems.

APOLOGIZE when you're wrong! Contrary to what some might think, this is never a sign of weakness. On the contrary, when you extend a deserved apology you develop a stronger image. It's easy to avoid responsibility, but it's professional to acknowledge missteps.

APPLY all the skills and talents you possess. And do it all the time. By working *at* something and *on* something, you'll make progress. Or, at least, you'll eliminate inappropriate options. That's progress! Then use what you have to move forward.

APPROACH all situations as if each one is the most important one in the world. In fact, each situation and option you face is, indeed, the most important one at that moment. Take action and make decisions because if you avoid them they will grow bigger and stronger. Maybe they'll grow to a size you can't handle. Then what will you do?

ASK questions whenever you face either old or new situations and options. All too often, people avoid asking questions because they think that it will be interpreted as being less than professional. "If I ask a question, people will know I don't know" is a feeling that can lead to an inferior image. Asking demonstrates confidence, interest, and professionalism.

ASSIST others as they climb their own career ladders. You never know when someone you help will be in a position to help you. It's easy to lend a hand to someone else, and such action is a sign of strength and confidence. None of us can go through life alone. Contribute – and accept – help even when it isn't requested.

ASSUME nothing! All too often, we think we know what a problem is and how to solve it. But that feeling is based only on our own experience – and we haven't experienced everything. It can be dangerous to assume that we know, or that others know, all the facts in any given situation. Work to gather the facts, but never take for granted you know what all of them are.

ASSURE others – and yourself – that you are acting in everyone's best interest. Be honest with yourself, and strive to keep others informed of your activities and positions. This will require open, honest communication, but it's the only way that you'll be able to function in a productive and supportive role.

ATTEND to the details. You know the old expression, "The devil is in the details." Big issues and opportunities are easy to see – for everyone. Leadership can be demonstrated by focusing on the details. When you cover the *little* things, the *big* things are much easier to handle.

ATTRACT as many "winners" as you can. A "winner" is someone who works at succeeding. He or she might not always succeed, but will always keep trying. When and if you surround yourself with such people, ideas and options will present themselves, and that will put you in a strong professional position. Look for those people who can help you. And be sure to help them whenever you can.

AUDIT your behaviors and attitudes, and those of others around you. Take a close and honest look at what is being done and at who's doing it. Measure priorities, identify reasons for a lack of priorities, and do it honestly. Use an imaginary "spread sheet" to list your assets and liabilities. Then make the necessary adjustments.

AVOID quick reactions. They might be wrong, and then you'll have additional problems to solve. There is no way to put a clock on "quick," because all situations are so different. But take that proverbial moment to "count to ten" before you react or respond. Do that when solutions seem to be good as well as when they seem to be bad. A moment of pause can lead to a long period of comfort.

BAIL out of bad situations. All too often, when people find themselves in an unpleasant or unproductive situation, they avoid taking the action necessary to correct the condition. When conditions are bad, get away from them – or fix them as soon as you can. But do it quickly. A boat will sink from even a tiny hole, if someone doesn't bail it out. When you find the "hole," fix it.

BALANCE all the elements of your life: family, job, hobbies, interests, and expectations. Inadequate focus on any one aspect at the cost of eliminating others will produce a shaky result. Without balance there will be chaos, and when priorities are confused the results will be diluted.

BELIEVE that you can do what you set out to do. Then do it! Too many people talk themselves out of trying new ideas or activities because they focus on "What if I can't do it?" Rather, focus on, "I can do this if I..." That shift in attitude will make all the difference in how you approach and evaluate options and opportunities. Take control!

BOLT out of the starting block. After you have made an assessment of conditions and options, move. Your initial consideration will help you identify direction, and once you have that, get moving! Your initial consideration will also help get you ready and set a course, but you won't get anywhere until you overcome inertia.

BOOST the value of others as quickly and as often as you can. There are too many workers and managers in business today who stand in the way of others and impede their actions. Don't fall into that category. Provide support, guidance, and direction to others, and they will probably come back to you in the future.

BORROW ideas from others – peers, subordinates, and superiors. No single individual with whom we have contact has a lock on information and ideas. Collaborative efforts usually produce better results than solitary activity. When you borrow, acknowledge and give credit. Doing otherwise is dishonest, as well as unethical. And it will come back to haunt you.

BRACE yourself for change. It's going to happen sooner or later. It always does. Nothing stays the same forever. It's easy to get comfortable in a situation, but you can't control all the elements that make up the situation. So be ready, and be prepared. You don't have to expect calamity or catastrophe, but don't expect unending stability either.

BRAND your product, your approach, and yourself. Develop and demonstrate all the factors that create the professional you. Decide how you want others to see and evaluate you. Everything about you will contribute to that "You." Just as a company works to establish a positive image (brand) of itself, you should do the same thing. Then sell the brand. It gets easier to sell as others become familiar with the brand – with "You."

BREAK old habits from time to time. Most of us do things because they "feel" good. Because they feel good, we keep doing them. That's what habits are all about – comfort. Now, there's nothing wrong with comfort, but be sure you're doing things in a particular way because you want to, not just because they feel good. Step out of your comfort zone from time to time, and see want happens.

BUILD relationships and positive associations. The simple fact of this verb is that it requires effort. Nothing can be built without effort. Waiting a long time for something to happen doesn't result in completion. Only activity leads to accomplishment. So work on these elements, factors, and people important to your personal and professional growth. Don't wait. Act.

BUY into opportunities. Do this actively. Be on the lookout for options that present themselves to you every day. A positive approach toward accepting new ideas and activities can lead to unexpected outcomes. Life can be like shopping at a flea market. You never know what will be there, but be observant and be ready to act quickly.

CALL upon others because you can't do everything yourself. The trick here, of course, is knowing whom to call, and that will come only if you constantly and consistently observe and evaluate those around you. Every one of us and our colleagues has strengths – and weaknesses. Only through observation will you be able to make the "right call."

CARE about the people around you. That means pay attention to them as individuals – not just as employees. Most of their lives, like yours, is spent away from the workplace so find out a bit about them, their interests, their expectations, and their concerns. When you demonstrate that you care about them, as people, they'll usually perform better for you. They care, too.

CATALOGUE the events taking place around you. Don't try to remember every single detail. That would be too difficult. Look for groupings to use: IT, HR, Security, Customer Service, etc. The patterns you observe will be helpful as your responsibilities expand and your options increase. You'll *see* more and not just *look* at developments. There is a big difference between *looking* and *seeing*!

CATCH everything that comes your way. Observe it. Measure it. Decide what, if anything, you want to do with it. Eventually, you might decide to discard it, but then it will be a conscious choice rather than a missed opportunity. Only when you know what *might be* of value can you interpret and incorporate it. Don't miss these opportunities!

CATER to those around you. That doesn't mean you have to be a servant. It means you pay attention to others and to what they need and want. When you pay attention, you'll be responsive and act for the benefit of those around you. This knowledge will help you lead because you will know the capabilities and the needs of your colleagues.

CELEBRATE the successes of others, not just your own. Acknowledgement and support will result in strong relationships with your colleagues. Support from them will then help you succeed, and success – everyone's – will lead to other success, yours and everyone else's. Try it. It's easy, and it's fun.

CHALLENGE yourself and others around you. That means moving out of the "Comfort Zone" we all have. Look for opportunities and options. Search for new growth and new challenges. Even after searching, if you're sure the "old way" was best for you, that's okay. That means you made a conscious decision, not just accepted whatever floated your way.

CHANGE what isn't working. There's more than one way to do everything. Most of us fall into comfortable habits and stay with them just because they *are* com-

fortable. Seek out options and alternatives. You can always go back to the old way, but if you do, it will be
because of more information, not just because of a
strong habit.

CHECK your progress constantly. Conditions change
every day, and you must measure, observe, and correct
if necessary. If you just assume everything is going
along just fine, you might drift into strange and uncomfortable situations. Correcting those situations usually
requires a lot more effort than a slight modification of
direction. Check on the "campfire" so it doesn't become
a "forest fire."

CHOOSE your battles carefully. Many of us are too
quick to "fix" everything and everyone around us. We
think we know what is best for everyone, and we're
quick to voice our opinions. Such action can grow very
tiresome for others, so don't voice every concern in every situation. You might be wrong. Focus your efforts,
and you're more likely to win the war.

CIRCULATE throughout your area of responsibility. In other words: get out of your office. When you're in your office, you can't see what's going on, and you can't talk to all the people you should. This doesn't mean you're "spying" on them. It's just good business and good sense to be out where the action is. So get out there!

CLEAN up all the details. Get rid of the fog. If your vision isn't clear, you can't be sure where you are or what obstacles might be in your way. If you want to take good pictures, be sure your lens is clean.

COACH those who report to you. That doesn't mean to just tell them what to do. It includes teaching them how to do it. And it requires continuous "in the moment" reaction and help. Don't simply wait until a task is completed to tell a staff member he or she did well – or poorly. Keep the dialogue going all the time.

COLLECT both facts and feelings from colleagues and customers. Because feelings drive behaviors, it's important to understand why people say and do the things they do. In order for you to respond appropriately you must understand both sides of the communication coin: facts and feelings.

COMBINE your talents with those of your colleagues. Joining forces with colleagues and allies will increase your perceptions of the world around you and how you can deal with opportunities and obstacles. You'll be far more effective with assistants on your side than you are alone.

COMPARE where you are with where you want to be. When you have a destination and a goal, you can use your internal business compass to get you there. If you don't have those two points clearly in mind (where you are and where you want to be), you'll just be guessing at what you have to do and what direction to take. Guessing can be very risky, time consuming, and costly.

COMPETE for the spotlight, but do it by sharing and concentrating on what *you* can do, not on what *others* can't do. Always take the high ground, but be sure to take it. Initiative will pay off, but false modesty or hesitance might cost you dearly.

COMMAND respect by treating others with respect. Regardless of the position you hold now or in the future, you'll always be dealing with other people – some of higher rank and some of lower rank. All people have the same basic desires and expectations. Show respect, and you'll get respect. Your "command presence" will warrant that respect from others.

CONFIDE in others who can help you. Ask for and accept assistance from others. Too many people have the "I'd rather do it myself" attitude. Now, independence is a good trait, but before you can get to a point where you can "do it," you'll need others to set up the conditions. None of us is completely alone or independent. We didn't get into this world by ourselves, so don't hesitate to let others help again.

CONSERVE what you don't need to use immediately. When opportunities are plentiful, we are often tempted to use everything at our disposal. Just be sure not to waste what *seems* to be an unending supply. When options appear boundless, set your own boundaries and use only what you need, not everything you have.

CONSIDER the ideas of others. What other people suggest might be different from your ideas, but they might be just as valid – and maybe even better than yours. But you'll never know if you shut down the flow of the discussion. Ultimately, your idea might be best, but if there's nothing to compare it with, you can't be certain.

CONTRADICT when necessary, but be positive in your approach. No one wants to be shown or be proven wrong about anything, but no one is perfect, either – even you. When you have an idea or a perception contrary to that of others, speak up and defend your position. But, that's the key: defend it with evidence, not just feelings.

CONTRAST what "is" and what "should be." If you are honest with yourself about those two conditions, it will be easy to see the differences. Once you see the differences, it will also be easy to determine how to reconcile them. First comes Contrast, then comes Clarity, then comes Commitment.

CONVERT potential to kinetic energy. Sounds like a page out of a high school physics textbook and, in a way, it is. Just thinking about doing something or going somewhere won't get you one inch closer to your goal. You must become active and "do" something. That's kinetic, and that's what gets results.

CORRECT your course when you discover you're going in the wrong direction. Now, that sounds obvious, but it will require that you constantly monitor your activity against your goals. That, too, sounds obvious, but many people don't do what they know they should do. Don't be one of "those people."

CREATE the conditions you need to be successful. If you don't have that clear vision we've described often, you might not even know what you need. Focus, identify, evaluate, and then create. You'll enhance your chances of succeeding every time.

CRUISE when it makes sense to follow the tide and move with the wind. You don't have to buck the prevailing winds and tides to make progress. This doesn't mean to simply "go along." It means to identify what your choices and strengths are and to use them to your advantage.

DEAL when necessary, but hold your ground when you are sure of your position. The only time to negotiate is when everything will be lost if you don't do it. Negotiating, by definition, means you will be giving up something g you want. Don't do that too quickly – only when it is absolutely necessary.

DEDICATE your time and talents to accomplishing a task. Actions are difficult only when you don't want to do them. When there is willingness, there is focus. Identify the task, define it, evaluate it. If it still makes sense after all that, do it.

DEFEND your core beliefs. In every business and professional relationship there will be differences of opinion. That's a good thing. But develop your core beliefs on the basis of experience and facts, and stand by them. We all know that certain things are the "right" things. I won't attempt to list them for you. Do that yourself. And then stand up for them, no matter what comes your way.

DEFINE the terms you use with colleagues and customers. Be sure they have the same understanding of the words as you do. Then check progress from time to time. If a misunderstanding goes uncorrected there is no way to predict where you'll end up. Don't take that chance.

DEFUSE conditions that get in the way of progress. In every human interaction there is the potential for misunderstanding. If such misunderstandings are not addressed and corrected when they are small, they certainly won't be when they are large. Take action quickly. Remember, it's much easier to put out a campfire than a forest fire.

DELEGATE to help others grow and to help yourself to "manage" rather than to "do." When you delegate a task to a staff person, be sure of 5 factors. 1) Let him or her know why he or she was selected. 2) Define the task. 3) Define the tools. 4) Let go! 5) Check in from time to time. Perhaps number 4 is the most difficult for most managers, but it is absolutely essential.

DELIVER what you promise. It makes no difference if you are talking about a product or a service. Be true to your word. Be realistic in your promises and commitments, and then stand behind them. All of us – and our companies – are evaluated on what we do, not by what we say we'll do. So do "it" when you make that promise.

DEMAND high caliber performance from yourself as well as from others. It's easy to see the faults and short-comings of those around you, but be aware that others are also evaluating you. You know what you can do – and what you should do – to be successful in your daily life. Just follow your own directions and expectations.

DESIGN a plan to get you where you want to go. It's like taking a trip in your car. If you don't know where you want to end up, it makes no difference which turns you make. In the end, though, all you will have accom-plished is using time and fuel. And you might then have to design another plan to get to where you wanted to go in the first place.

DESIGNATE who should do what when. Then, if at all possible, let the designated person determine the "how." You may know how you would accomplish a specific task, but that's only one way. There are many ways to reach a goal. Give others who report to you the chance to decide how to reach a goal. Monitor the person, of course, but let him find his own way.

DETERMINE priorities and sequences before you start a project. The up-front thinking time and activity is the least expensive part of any project. It's cheap and easy to erase or delete a line from a plan, but it's expensive to tear down a wall when you decide it's in the wrong place.

DEVELOP relationships wherever you can, but be sure they are positive relationships. You can do that by observing yourself as others observe you. Be honest with yourself. What you might intend to be seen as a positive trait might be seen as a negative by others. Put yourself in the shoes of other people and observe yourself. What do you see? Do you like it?

DEVOTE all of your talents to any task. This is simply another way of looking at the need to focus on a destination or a goal in order to reach it. If you are distracted, you might miss opportunities and not see pitfalls. That can lead to unnecessary detours and lost time. Time is a non-renewable commodity. Don't waste it.

DIAGNOSE all the symptoms of a situation. Look at, in, around, and under a situation before you take any action. All too often, a brief glance or observation leaves out details that are important to the success of a project. This goes for people, too. Look at your staff and your customers from every possible perspective before you make a judgment.

DIFFERENTIATE between what "feels" good and what "is" good. Only then will you be able to do the right thing with consistency and focus. The world provides many paths you might follow, but the choices will be clear only if you take careful note of the differences each provides. Act with care rather than on impulse.

DILUTE the tension you experience in the workplace and at home. If anything goes unchecked or unattended, it could reach a point of no return. Be aware constantly of the changing conditions around you and take the initiative to "calm down" potential difficulties. A small amount of something can be acceptable, but a concentrated amount could be disastrous.

DISCUSS possibilities and options with those around you, both colleagues and family. You probably have a specific idea of how something should be done, for example, but there might be other ways to accomplish the task, ways you hadn't even considered. Talk about the options – and listen to the suggestions of others. You just might discover something new.

DISMISS what can't be fixed. This applies to people and projects. When a problem exists with a product or a service, identify the cause and make adjustments. If the adjustments don't fix the problem, perhaps the product or service was inappropriate in the first place. Move on! Help others to grow, but if they don't – or won't, perhaps that initial selection, too, was inappropriate. Move on!

DISPLAY what you have acquired and accomplished. Likewise, what you still seek and desire. Don't hide your accomplishments, but on the other hand, don't taunt others with your gains. When others can see what you have done, that observation can serve as a guide and an inspiration for them. So help them.

DIVERSIFY to improve and to gain, not just to look different. If you have only one product or one talent, you are at the mercy of the whims of others. The proverbial "one trick pony" can and will be replaced when another "trick" appears. Look for – and try out – multiple options. If one fails, you'll still have plenty of others to use.

DIVEST yourself of unnecessary baggage. Get rid of what you don't need. You can do this by taking an honest inventory of what is important to you – really important. Evaluating "things" vs. "people" vs. "values," for example, will tell you what to keep and cultivate and what to discard. You can't keep everything, so choose what you want and need.

DIVIDE your time between work and family. Both are important to you, and it's important to nurture both. Everything changes as time passes, and your relationships will change. So take care. Don't sacrifice one part of your life for the others. Plan your time, and all those you touch will be pleased and gratified because they will be respected. So will you.

DONATE some of what you have in order to help others with whom you come in contact: staff, customers, and family. This doesn't mean giving away goods or money. It means sharing what you have so that others can learn and benefit from your experience and knowledge. If you are in a position to manage others, what you give to them will be returned in kind. What do you want from others? Do you give it to them?

DRAW lines where necessary. It is often tempting to try to do everything – or to let everything just happen. That will only lead to chaos and confusion. Everyone needs direction, even if they prefer a certain view. Be the one to set those directions. You'll help others, and yourself, to grow and develop by design rather than by happenstance.

DRIVE yourself – and others – to succeed, but do it with caution. Set limits, but move forward. If there isn't motivation and drive, there will probably be stagnation, or worse – regression. Take the initiative. Pick a target, select the tools, and move forward.

EARN respect by showing respect. Most things in life don't just show up unexpectedly. They take time and work. Showing respect is usually easy if we look for and concentrate on the positive contributions of those around us. When we do that, in most cases, people will respond in kind, and we will have earned respect just by doing the right thing.

EDUCATE yourself in a wide variety of fields and interests. You'll probably focus on a primary area of interest, of course, but when you learn about other parts of life, you'll find that the primary area will be expanded by the variables offered by the other areas. Like adding spices or aromas to an environment, that portion of the world is still primary but the addition modifies it. And you can always change those modifiers.

ELECTRIFY your day – every day. Talk to yourself and ask a few questions at the start of every day. Questions like: What can I accomplish today? Where should I focus my attention? Why am I here today? Who can I help? Just these few examples can contribute to forming your day, every day. Add your own and see what happens.

ENCOURAGE those who report to you to take on new tasks and responsibilities. Help then grow. But be sure that you give them the tools and the support they'll need to achieve their goals. Don't just "throw them in the water and expect them to swim out" on their own. Encourage, but support and help when necessary.

ENERGIZE those around you by giving them permission and encouragement – permission to try new things and the support to accomplish them. As a manager and/or as a parent you have the opportunity and the responsibility to help others learn. Make learning exciting, and they'll keep asking you for more. What a contribution you can then make!

ENGAGE the world and everything in it. Be open to new experiences on the job, in your family, and in your private life. Participate, don't just observe or react. You'll see opportunities only when you open yourself to them. Engage. Observe. Explore. Grow. There is much to be learned and much to contribute if you are open and responsive.

ENJOY life. Sounds simplistic, doesn't it? But, all too often, we lose sight of the fact that life is precious and exciting. Focus on the good, look for the good, and you'll find it. A colleague of mine says, "Don't focus on the 'hole,' add the letter 'W,' and make the word 'whole.'" Good advice for all of us.

ENTER into each new challenge and opportunity with the attitude that says, "I can do this, and I'll do it as well as I can." In some situations, time and conditions will make success difficult, perhaps impossible, but that's okay. You tried. You learned. Now move on to a new challenge. Life is full of these if you just look for them.

ENTERTAIN the ideas and suggestions that come from others. They might be better than yours, or they might complement them. In either case, the end product or result will be better because of the cooperation and openness. If you insulate yourself, you'll isolate yourself. Expand and embrace.

EVALUATE what you have accomplished when you come to the end of every day. Take stock, and keep score on yourself. Ask yourself a few questions like: How did I grow today? Who did I help? What's left to do? Add your own. No one else will see your score, but your private results will help you – and by extension – help others too.

EXCHANGE old habits that are tired and don't work so well any more for new ones. We all get comfortable doing the same things the same way over and over. But new options are always available. Look for them, and try them out for a while. It's like putting on a new pair of shoes, though. You have to walk around in them for a while before they feel comfortable. Of course, you can always go back to the old shoes – or habits – if you get blisters.

EXCITE your colleagues, students, or family by opening up their worlds to new opportunities and new adventures. They don't have to be big, just interesting and new. If you position the newness as a chance to grow and explore, you'll create the excitement for them. Of course, you must do the same thing for yourself, or others won't believe or follow you. Lead – don't preach.

EXHAUST all possibilities and options before accepting defeat or acknowledging failure. That means trying new and different methods with each successive attempt. Don't just keep doing the same thing that didn't work in the first place and expect a different outcome. That just doesn't work, and it wastes a lot of time.

EXPAND your world by taking the initiative and by taking chances. We have all been dealt a "hand" by circumstances, but it's up to us to either accept what we were handed or to take action to change those circumstances. Easy to say, but it takes a lot of work. Get started. Read a book, enroll in a course, take a trip, build something. But get started!

FABRICATE when you don't have ready-made items. This should include not only the "things" you need in your daily work, but also the techniques and tactics you need to work successfully with your colleagues and customers. Be creative after you have been observant. Use what you have, and then make what you need.

FACE the facts in all situations. Often it's easy – and tempting – to see things as we wish they were rather than as what they actually are. Such self-deception, however, can lead to wasted time and false starts. Concentrate on "what is," then you can work on making it what you want it to be.

FEATURE all the members of your staff. Let them shine. And be sure all their colleagues recognize their accomplishments. Frequently, managers just expect good performance but don't acknowledge it openly. Shine the spotlight where it belongs – on producers – not on the non-performers who get attention through discipline.

FEEL what your colleagues feel as much as you possibly can. Because feelings drive behaviors, your awareness of how your staff feels about situations will help you understand the things you see them do. When you understand their motivations, you'll be able to compliment or correct with accuracy. It works at home too.

FILTER out the unimportant. All messages don't carry the same weight. People, timing, and locations can strengthen or weaken the impact and importance of information you receive from others, at home or at work. Listen, balance, and process before you conclude.

FIND opportunities, and explore them. You never know where they might lead. That requires activity and attention. Many people "look" at situations, but others "see" them. There is a great deal of difference between "looking" and "seeing." Be a "seer" not a "looker." Be sure you recognize the opportunities that come your way.

FINISH whatever you start. Sometimes finishing just means deciding that what you've been doing doesn't work. If you planned, monitored, and evaluated, you might conclude an activity is not going to turn out as you had expected or planned. If that's the case, stop and move on to other opportunities.

FIRE the people who won't do what is necessary for the benefit of the organization. In the book on managing that I coauthored a couple of years ago, my colleague and I made a point that a manager should be like a gardener. On the positive side, the gardener must pick the seeds, tend the soil, and control the environment to the extent possible. On the negative side of gardening, when the weeds come up they must be pulled out. Poor performing staff people can be like weeds. Get rid of them!

FIX problems as soon as you identify them. If you wait for someone else to do the fixing or hope the problem will fix itself, you'll be disappointed. Waiting doesn't work. Problems usually start small, and then they grow – sometimes very quickly. A small leak in a dike can be fixed easily. If it is ignored, the dike will breach. Then you have a mega-problem. Don't let that happen.

FOCUS on the goal, not on the potholes. Life is filled with decisions we must make, but good decisions are possible only when you have sufficient information. Even with information, without a destination, you might use up the resources at your disposal without getting where you want to go. You'll use up all your time and fuel and not get to where you want to be. Don't run out of gas.

FOLLOW your instincts, but monitor the consequences of your behavior. When you give sufficient thought to developing plans, careful execution will produce the benefits you want. The important element here is the simple fact that any progress requires you to take careful aim and then work toward the goals you set.

FOLLOW UP on the activities and progress of your staff. One of the primary duties of a manager is to delegate responsibilities and tasks to others in the organization. But that doesn't mean just giving orders and walking away, hoping the others will do what you directed them to do. You must check progress, smooth out the bumps when necessary, and, finally, recognize and reward the progress. That works well with your family relationships, too.

FORM plans and strategies before starting any project. Impatience can be a major problem for high-energy people who want to get things done. So use that energy at the outset to select your course of action. A little up-front planning will help guarantee positive outcomes.

FUND your ideas with the resources they need. This doesn't relate only to money. Of course, that kind of funding is often necessary, but there are other funds you can donate to family and staff. Time, attention, advice, support, and empathy are all solid currency and can pay huge dividends when properly invested.

GATHER the resources available to you, before you initiate any action, to be sure you have what you need. Don't begin until you're ready to begin. Being ready is part attitude and part inventory. Be sure you have both.

GENERATE ideas and opportunities by asking questions of yourself and of others. Don't wait for things to just come to you. They might – if you're lucky – but, more often, you have to work for what you want. Look for: What could be? Why? How? or Why not? Be inquisitive all the time, and you might change the world.

GESTURE to support your words. That doesn't mean waving your arms around just to make a point. It means to be sure that your total behavior supports your ideas and beliefs. Talk is cheap, (We've all heard that.), but actions demonstrate the person behind the words. "Show" what you believe, don't just talk about it.

GET AWAY from daily pressures every once in a while to recharge your internal batteries and get a fresh perspective on your situation – and your problems. If you stay in the midst of a situation, in time, you won't be able to see it clearly. Step away, reassess, revise, and then revisit. The fresh perspective will eventually give you new insights.

GET READY. Get set. Go! Remember that from when you were a child? The sequence is very important. Get ready by doing your research and fact-finding. Get set by building your plan after evaluating your options. Go only after taking those first two steps. "Going" without prepping is risky – and dangerous. Stack the deck in your favor.

GRASP opportunities when they present themselves. Now, they won't tap you on the shoulder and say, "Here I am." You have to keep your antennae up and be aware when they start to vibrate. The trick is to recognize that opportunities are within your reach. Then reach out, grab them, and make them your own.

GAUGE the potential for success and/or failure. If you stay alert, observe, and measure the conditions around you – on the job and in the community – you'll be able to identify targets of opportunity and areas of danger. That measurement will help you navigate a productive course.

GUIDE those who report to you and depend upon you. When you are in a leadership position, realize that others are looking for guidance and direction, and they are looking directly at you. They are evaluating everything you do to, with, and for them. Help them learn to grow. Give them the benefits of what you have already learned. Don't make them work too hard getting information from you. Give them the gift of yourself.

HARVEST the crops you plant and take care that what you planted was, indeed, what you wanted because that's what you'll get. You can't plant daisies and expect to see roses. The conditions and the reputation you plant will come back to you whether you like it or not. Remember the old adage. "As you sow, so shall you reap." That's always how it works so be careful what you plant.

HELP, wherever you can, whomever you can. Do that for two reasons. First, it's a good and professional way to relate to others. That's part of your job and your responsibility. Second, that helpful behavior could very well come back to you. None of us knows when conditions will change, and those we help might be in positions to help us in the future. That's a good trade and a good payback.

HEAR what others are telling you. Really *hear* it! Be active when you relate to others. Pay attention. Now that might seem obvious and, in many respects, it is, but while many people are physically present in a discussion, they are mentally on vacation. When those who report to you talk, listen to what they have to say. It's important to them or they wouldn't say it. And what they have to say might turn out to be very important for you!

HESITATE until you're sure about what you want to say or do. Often, it's tempting – and it feels good – to "sound off" or to "shoot from the hip." Just remember, once the words are spoken, or the actions are taken, you can't set the clock back for a second try if the first one didn't work well. A brief pause at the front end can save a lot of time at the concluding stages of any activity.

HIGHLIGHT what is most important to you and don't lose sight of it. We're all bombarded with a variety of opportunities and problems, so we have to set priorities. Look at what is in front of you and decide what you must do first, second, third, etc. It's your choice, so choose and stick with your choice. If you learn, eventually, that the choice was incorrect or inappropriate, make another choice, and move on.

HIRE the people who can do what needs to be done and are willing to do it. Those are two very significant criteria, but there is a third one that is often overlooked in the hiring process. Be sure that the new people will fit into your organization. Check on the personal qualities that will help a candidate fit into the existing structure. If the candidate doesn't fit but is hired on the basis of the first two criteria, you and the candidate are sure to have trouble.

HOLD on to the techniques and the plans that work, but always look at new developments. Successful organizations often run into difficulty because they "hold on" to a process or a belief, long after changing conditions have changed their value. Be sure you retain selected behaviors and beliefs because they "are" good, not just because they "feel" good.

HONOR the needs, desires, and expectations of others in your family and on the job. You have a certain perspective of the elements in your world, and you're entitled to it. But so is everyone else entitled to his or her perspectives. What others see and want might not be the same as your choices, but theirs are as valid as yours. Look at them. You might learn something new you can use.

HOPE to be successful, but don't let hope be your strategy. Hope translates to doing nothing, and you'll lose control if you simply sit and wait for things to come your way. You must take action. Look for opportunities and change tactics when appropriate. Measure and evaluate. Then proceed, or change your plan on the basis of what you observe.

IMAGINE what you can achieve if no obstacles stand in your way. Then look at those obstacles and determine if they are truly obstacles or just inconveniences. If they turn out to be inconveniences, go around them or ignore them, and let your imagination lead you to new vistas. Never talk yourself out of a good idea.

IMPRESS others with action, not words. Words are fleeting, but the impact of action remains for a long time. We all form impressions of others by what they "do." If and when you determine how you want others to think of you, be sure to act in ways that will foster that impression. You can't get inside someone and push his or her "impressions" button, but you can control your behavior and, by doing that, create an impression in others.

IMPROVE the product you create and the techniques you use. You can always find a "better way" because the perfect solution for anything hasn't been found yet – and never will be found. Keep asking yourself – and others – "How can we do this better?" If you keep doing something over and over in the same way because you

feel you are "in a groove," in time you might find yourself "in a rut." Very different. It's your choice!

IMPROVISE when there isn't a clear-cut method already spelled out. In most situations you can't wait for
the perfect conditions to present themselves before you
take action. When the "perfect conditions" don't exist,
be creative. That doesn't mean be careless. Quite the
contrary! Being creative requires one to look carefully
at a situation, measure the degree of "perfection," and
then "make up" what has to be done to get as close as
possible to that image of real perfection.

INCLUDE every appropriate member of a group. It's
easy to overlook some members of a group (work or
family) if you're in a hurry. Include not only the ones
who are close at the moment, but also those who will
participate in or be affected later by your decisions. Inclusion up front is always better than explanation later.

INCORPORATE divergent points of view in decision-making. All of us have preferences and biases in how we approach situations, and often those biases have a strong influence on how we perceive "facts." The perception others have of those same "facts" might change your course of action. Look at those various options early and avoid later patchwork.

INCREASE the contributions of others by increasing your inclusion of them and by showing your interest in their potential contributions. Ask, listen, evaluate, and then synthesize. The combined contribution of many will usually outweigh the impact of only a few. You have nothing to lose by expanding input.

INSPIRE others by giving credit and praise where it's due. It takes only a moment to acknowledge the talents and contributions of those around you, but that moment will last a long time in the minds of the ones you praised. Focus on the positive actions of others rather than on their errors or shortcomings. Their performance will rise to meet your expectations.

INTEGRATE various points of view and perceptions as you navigate through your responsibilities and decisions. This doesn't mean that you'll have to give up your authority. It means that you'll have more information at your disposal. More information produces better data, which produces clearer perceptions, which produce better choices. Nice chain of events.

INTERCEDE on the part of those who need assistance. As a manager and a leader, you are in a position to help others who can benefit from your experience and influence. Give the help freely, but don't jump into every situation that comes up. Observe, evaluate, and then contribute your talents and experience. When the time comes, others might do this for you. Give the gift of time and attention, and they will come back to you.

INTERPRET what might seem complicated to others who are not as familiar with a topic as you are. Newcomers to your staff might need assistance in understanding what you learned over time. Save them time by "speaking a language" they will understand as they grow into their new roles.

INTRODUCE new ideas and procedures with appropriate information. Just giving directions or "orders," without including appropriate background data, makes following them difficult. As a leader, you are a teacher, so be sure to help your "pupils" learn what they need to know. Often, they not only need to know "what" is needed, they also need to know "why" it's needed.

INVEST in others. Your staff and your family are your legacy. Devoting time and attention to them on a regular basis will produce strong dividends in the future. It's like investing your money. A little bit at a time, over time, produces surprising results.

INVESTIGATE what you don't understand. Be open to new ideas and suggestions, but also to questions. And you should ask question, too. Continue to look for improvement in procedures and services by looking for better ways to deliver them. Be comfortable, but don't become complacent.

INVITE others to contribute ideas and suggestions. Be sure the invitations are extended to everyone who can help: colleagues, staff, superiors, and, most importantly, your customers. All too often managers hesitate to ask for ideas because they think that this indicates incompetence and a lack of knowledge. Just the opposite is true. Try it, and see what the reaction is.

ISOLATE comments, particularly criticism and objections. Be sure you know exactly what is important to clients and staff. If you don't know, you might spend too much time and effort solving the wrong problems. Only when you are sure what the problem really is, can you address it.

ISSUE communication on a consistent and predictable schedule. When you establish a pattern of behavior in this area your staff – and perhaps your clients – will come to look forward to the information. You'll be able to establish a productive communication link that will serve you – and others – well
JOIN in discussions and debates. Don't "blend into" the furniture. Be seen and be heard. Be polite, but don't

wait for an invitation to participate. Others might not know your interests, and they might not want to embarrass you. Don't take the chance of being overlooked. Take the initiative.

JUDGE actions – everyone's, yours as well as your staff's, customers' and clients'. This doesn't mean finding fault. It means measuring and evaluating. Your conclusions about the actions of others might be positive. If so, good. If they are negative, decide what action you have to take to turn them in a different direction.

JUSTIFY your time, energy, and interest by demonstrating results. Do what is expected of you – and a little more – and you'll see quickly how others respond. Words are easy. That's why we use them so quickly. But actions demonstrate, and that's what gets others to act and react.

KICK START your intentions and your plans. Too often people talk themselves out of a good idea. They focus on "What if I can't do it?" rather than "What do I have to do?" Don't waste your time and talent asking the wrong question. Get started. Now!

KINDLE any creative and productive flames you detect. In most organizations you'll find people who are dynamic and outgoing. They are easy to detect and to involve. It's the quiet, retiring ones who are the challenge. Help them reach their potential by providing the fuel (encouragement and support) necessary to "set them on fire."

KNOW what you want to accomplish. Know where you are and where you want to go. When you identify those two points, your next logical and necessary step is plotting your course. There are many different ways to reach a destination, but first you have to know exactly what your destination is. Without that knowledge you might use up a lot of time and energy but not get where you want to go.

LAUNCH ideas and activities with deliberation. Don't wait for things to "just happen." They usually don't. Take the initiative. Launching a boat, a plane, or an idea requires focused effort. Once you overcome inertia, the vehicle almost takes on a life of its own. It "will" move. Your task – your responsibility – is to see that it moves in the right direction.

LEAD in the direction you want everyone to go. Take a position, and take action. When you're "out front," others will follow because they see you setting the example. Clear demonstration is usually much stronger and more efficient than giving directions. Remember the adage: "Actions speak louder than words." It's true, and it works!

LEAN on others for support. There's nothing wrong or weak in using others to support your position. Certainly that doesn't mean taking advantage of others. It reflects the idea that mutual support can produce collectively what individual actions cannot. When you look for such support, you'll demonstrate to others that you respect and value them, their participation, and their help.

LEAP over obstacles. They're all around you, but look at them from two perspectives. They can be either inhibitors or encouragers. If they are inhibitors, you might stay fenced in, limited, lost. If they are encouragers, you'll look for the opportunities and the gaps in the barriers. You'll find a way over, around, or through, but you won't stay "cooped up."

LEAVE the things you can't influence or change. There are plenty of opportunities in the world where you can focus your attention. When you encounter something you can't change, look for other opportunities where you can have an impact. After successfully completing those, you can always return for another look at what seemed impossible. The changing conditions might result in changing options.

LEND a helping hand whenever you can to whomever needs it. When you find yourself in a position to help someone, take it. Your actions will be noticed, and remembered, and you never know when that other person can return the favor. When you provide assistance, you'll receive it.

LIMIT the number of activities you pursue during any given day. You can't do everything! Only you can determine how many activities are enough – or too many – but use good judgment. As tempting as it is to try to do everything, it doesn't work. Look at and determine priorities, and then get going. Leave the other options for another day. They'll wait.

LIST your priorities. And, really, make a list! Write down on paper or on your computer what is important to you. The physical act of writing is a great discipline. If you can't write your ideas, they aren't clear in your mind. And if they aren't clear, how can you proceed with any expectation of success?

LISTEN to what others have to say. You don't know everything (yet), and you never will. Take advantage of what others know and can offer to you. Their knowledge, experience, and expectations might just be the elements you need to be successful. Multiple ingredients, when combined well, produce interesting results. Ask any chef!

LOCATE the options and the obstacles. And then look for the people who can help you successfully accomplish your tasks. This requires action on your part. You must actively seek the ideas, talents, and interests of those around you. Many people "hide their lights under a basket" because they are unsure of themselves and their possible contributions. Look for those people. Help them. It will help you, too.

LOOK around you. What do you see? "Around" is the key word here. Look in all directions because you'll never know what you'll find "out there." Too often, managers look in only one direction – ahead. That's okay in some situations, of course, but if that's the only vision you have, you might be blindsided by someone or something on your flank. If that happens, you'll be knocked off course, and you won't be successful. Don't take that risk.

MAINTAIN a steady balance. Your core values are important here. Ask yourself what drives and what motivates you. What is important to you? Speed and direction can be changed quickly and often as long as you stay balanced. When you lose your balance, you'll fall, or you'll flounder. All the others who stay balanced will pass you. And you might never catch up to them.

MANAGE all the elements under your control: people, funds, and facilities. This requires active and constant participation on your part. You must take control and make adjustments to stay on course. If you don't manage, you'll simply react, and you'll miss opportunities others might identify.

MANEUVER to get into the best position to achieve what is important to you. As with so many elements in your business or personal worlds, various forces pull from all directions. Moving through and around those forces will allow you to succeed. Just as a ship's captain or an airline pilot adjusts course to account for winds and tides, you can, and must, do the same.

MANIPULATE all the elements under your control. Often, managers "inherit" situations that have worked –

or not worked – in the past. Resist the temptation to continue the status quo. Look for ways, people, and resources that will assist you in improving and developing the workplace conditions. Change for the sake of change, of course, isn't good, but not changing for the sake of not changing isn't good, either.

MARKET yourself, your ideas, and your vision. Rarely will others be spokespeople for you. Also, no one else knows you as well as you do. So let the world (big or small) know what you can do and how valuable you are. Nothing ever got sold without some effort. Use that effort on yourself.

MEASURE your progress – and the progress of those around you. Without numbers and other specifics, it's impossible to be sure you're making progress. Figure out the measurement scale you need, teach others about it, and apply it. Others will catch on to this habit also, and then everyone will recognize what's happening – or not happening!

MEET regularly with all the people you work with. Get to know them as people, not just as employees. "On the job" is only a part of their lives. If you know about the other parts, you can have a great influence on their job productivity. So schedule those times to meet! One more thing. Take the initiative to schedule times to meet with your boss. Don't wait for your boss to get the idea. You do it!

MODIFY what you're doing if those actions aren't producing the results you want. Every one of us is predisposed to do what "feels" good, but sometimes what feels good isn't productive. Try new approaches, look for innovative methods, and experiment. Keep at it because conditions – the whole world – keep changing, and only modifications can help you keep up with those changes.

MOLD your staff into a cohesive and productive team. Identify, seek out, and capitalize on the multiple talents that you find within your staff. Distribute the responsibilities after determining when and how they can be distributed and best carried out to build your team. The world will change as conditions change, but that's okay.

There is a dynamic process which mixes materials and ingredients. Combine and refine for success.

MONITOR everything around you. By staying constantly alert you'll see – not just look at – opportunities and challenges. You'll be able to act with purpose and direction. If you don't see what's around you, you'll get surprised by the unexpected. Watch, question, and modify.

MOVE to stay well positioned. If you remain still, the world will pass you by. Nothing on Earth, certainly in the workplace, remains static. Expect and embrace change, as long as you change with the conditions. This doesn't mean compromising your principles or core beliefs. It means realizing how you can, and should, incorporate them in the evolving world of work, home, and community.

MODEL the behaviors you want your staff to demonstrate. Telling, of course, is good; but behavior really shows the truth about people. What you do – good or bad – is probably what your staff will do. "Show" is always stronger and more effective than "Tell."

NAVIGATE carefully through all the "minefields" that might present themselves during your day. The people and events that fill your workday and social life can bring surprises. Always keep two checkpoints in mind: where you are now, and where you what to go. If you don't have both of those points, you won't be able to chart a course.

NOTICE the reactions you get. Pay attention to what is going on around you all the time. What you do, what you say, and how you say and do it will produce reaction in those around you. If you don't see – really see – and hear – really hear, you won't have the feedback you need to be sure you are accomplishing what you intend.

NOTIFY those around you of what needs to be done. All too often we assume others will "figure out" what we want, why we want it, and how we want it to be done. Don't assume! If you're wrong, you haven't helped others, and you might even find yourself getting angry because the others didn't respond the way you wanted. Tell them!

OBSERVE everything around you. This doesn't mean to just look at things. Be sure you see them. There is a world of difference between *looking* and *seeing*. The first is physical, but the second in intellectual. The second will help you move forward without stumbling.

OBTAIN as much data as you can before making decisions. Look, ask questions, revise. Take advantage of the knowledge of others. Trial and error might be okay in some arenas, but it certainly is costly, wasteful, and time-consuming.

OPEN the doors and windows of information. Open dialogue with colleagues. Take the initiative. Don't wait for someone else to open a conversation or a line of inquiry. When you take the initiative, you might be pleasantly surprised at what turns up.

OPERATE all the systems you have available to you. Learn how to use all the tools you have at your disposal. Your experiences will be focused and tempered by exposure to others and their experiences. You don't have to learn everything from "scratch." Build on what others have already learned.

ORCHESTRATE all of your activities. That means have a plan and know what tools can do what job. The conductor of an orchestra knows the abilities and limitations of every instrument in his orchestra. That knowledge, coupled with a musical score, enables him to "make music." You can do that, too, if you know your orchestra and what they can – or can't – do. Of course, as the manager, you have to provide the "musical score."

OVERCOME the common tendency to "play it safe." If you never take a chance or take a step forward, you'll never get anywhere. You'll be stuck! Often, it's frightening to take that first step in a new direction, but it's absolutely necessary if you expect to make any progress at all.

PACE yourself at all times in all endeavors. You can't work at high speed all the time. Take inventory of your progress and, if you're not progressing as you want, it might be because you're going in the wrong direction, and not because you're moving too slowly. High speed isn't always the most productive pace.

PARTICIPATE in all the aspects of your work world. If you aren't a "player," you won't experience all the excitement – and frustration – reflected in your world. If you are only an observer, you'll deprive yourself of experiences that might be of value in your business, social, and family lives.

PAUSE and take a breath. Look around. It's impossible to be moving all the time. You need to recharge your batteries or they'll die. Also, growth occurs during periods of rest. So take a break, look around, evaluate developments and then you'll be ready to move again.

PAY the debts you owe to others. This isn't about money, although that too is certainly important. It's about returning favors and acknowledging contributions of associates. No one works in a vacuum, so be sure to "balance your business and social books."

PAY ATTENTION to your fellow workers to be sure you understand what they want, need, and expect. They are important for the success of your department or business. But even more importantly, pay attention to your customers and all the people who use your services or products. Without them, there's nothing else!

PERFORM at the highest level you can achieve and sustain. The world responds and judges on the basis of what you do, not what you say you will do. Talk isn't cheap, as some people say. It's worthless if it isn't supported by action, and it's easy for others to see your actions. Those actions speak for themselves.

PERSIST in moving toward your goals. You have to keep at it, or you'll lose ground. Nothing stands still. Even Alice in Wonderland learned that when she was told by the Queen, "You have to keep running as fast as you can just to keep up. If you want to get someplace, you have to run twice as fast."

PINPOINT your targets, your opportunities, and your obstacles. If you don't identify them during the business day, you'll stubble. When you're falling, it's hard to keep focused on an objective. When you eliminate distractions, you'll be able to keep that all-important focus.

PLAN how you're going to get from point A to point B. Of course, you'll be the one to identify the two points, but be sure you identify them clearly. If you don't have both points identified, clearly you won't be able to plan or follow an accurate course. You'll just drift, and that's costly!

PLAY with ideas. Look for options. Explore new ways to accomplish tasks under your responsibility. Break out of the comfort zone we all feel. Approach a task – even a familiar one –as if you've never encountered it before. If it's brand new, and you aren't locked in to any certain way of behaving, what can you do? Try a new action, and see what happens.

PLEASE the people around you. That doesn't mean you have to fawn over them or patronize them. It means to respect them. Treat them well. It's the Golden Rule. You'll always get better responses and results with respect than with control.

PRACTICE what you'll say when you are facing a pressure or tense situation, like a presentation, a performance review, or delegating a task. The words you use, and the way you say them will carry and create a lasting impression. Be sure it's the impression you want. Don't leave that impression to chance. Rehearse!

PRAISE others at every opportunity you have. It doesn't have to be flowery, just specific, honest, and timely. A basic principle of one school of behavioral psychology says to acknowledge positive behavior and ignore negative behavior. Because everyone wants to be acknowledged, the positive behavior will increase.

PRAY not only to get help, but also to discover ways to give it. It seems that most people look for that "divine intervention" when they are in trouble or in need. Of course, there's nothing wrong with asking for assistance, but look for ways you can provide that assistance to others, too. You might have exactly what those others might need, so ask for that direction. Giving help to others is a great way to pay back for what you have already received.

PREPARE for all kinds of options. You can never be sure what will come your way so be aware, be flexible, and be ready. If you remain constantly alert to your surroundings and to your colleagues, you'll minimize surprises and be able to flow with the changes. Be adaptable, and you'll be successful.

PRESENT both directives and options to those around you. Let them know what you expect from them – and what they can expect from you. One of the greatest contributors to discontent is misinformation. Even worse – no information. Don't contribute to that situation.

PRESERVE what's working and change what isn't. Always be alert to new possibilities, but resist the temptation to change for change sake – or to change just to make an impression on others around you. Tradition can be good – and productive. Use it, but don't be bound by it.

PREVENT errors by providing information and assistance. All too often managers become focused on their own perspectives, and they forget the needs of the others working with them. From your perspective you can see the work world far more clearly and broadly than others can. Use that perspective to help the others around you.

PRIORITIZE your actions and model that for others. You can't do everything yourself, so make choices based on what you know must be done. Take care of first things first. When others see what you're doing, and why, they'll follow suit.

PROBE to get to the reasons, the questions, and the problems. All too often we are tempted to "jump right in" and "fix" something. But often, we discover the wrong "something." Quick example. When we hear a customer say something like, "Too expensive," we often react with an adjusted price. Don't just react. Probe to find out exactly what "too expensive" really means to the customer. It might be quite different from what you expect. Ask your own questions before you volunteer new information.

PROCESS information. Take your time. Don't jump to a quick conclusion. Be sure of facts, feelings, and options before presenting a solution. A few moments delay can save hours of repair.

PRODUCE as well as you can. Whether it's a product or a service, take the time and use the talent available. If you can't "do it" alone (and you probably can't), find others who can help. Enlist that help. Acknowledge it. And reward it. Everybody will benefit.

PROJECT outward and forward. Don't just reflect on that past. Certainly, considering and evaluating past experiences are necessary, but what lies ahead is most important. You can only reflect on the past, but you can influence the future – if you give it focused and sufficient thought and attention.

PROMOTE both people and ideas. They go hand in hand. When you are convinced a new idea has merit, enlist the support and cooperation of others to help.

When you all experience success, move those who helped you to higher levels. As a manager, be a teacher and help others grow.

PROTECT the image that will encourage others to be confident in you and be comfortable with your leadership ability. Such an image will grow relationships and expand cooperation. Everything you say and do contributes to that image, so be sure you don't ignore or jeopardize it by being careless.

PROVE to yourself – and to others – that you can and do make good decisions. Take chances, but only those chances that have been carefully considered and evaluated. When you take your time, you'll make fewer errors, and you'll convince yourself, and others, that you can truly lead and manage.

PROVIDE options and opportunities for those who work with and for you. In many respects, you exert strong influence and control over many other people.

Don't "control," but rather "teach," "counsel," and "support." You can do what they can't. You can broaden their horizons and their entire worlds if you want to!

PUBLISH what you know, what you think, and what you feel. This doesn't mean you have to write a book, but you can produce a newsletter, a blog, or just a good e-mail. Broaden your contacts by using these tools in addition to the usual face-to-face conversations. Published materials often take on a life of their own. Contribute to that life.

PULL others along as you grow and develop. Many people are content with what they have and are unsure about trying new things. As a manager, open their eyes to new options. Show them how they can achieve new heights, and then pull them out of their comfortable "ruts." Help them explore and grow, even when they aren't sure about trying that.

PUSH your staff into new arenas and new experiences. Change can be frightening for some people and, consequently, they remain in a comfortable place. They resist change because it's uncertain. As a manager, encourage them to expand, to take risks (acceptable risks), and then support their efforts. Keep them from failing, of course, but get them to try something new.

QUANTIFY and be specific about it. If you don't put numbers and measurements against your efforts, you'll never know for certain how you're doing. A "little," a "lot," "some," a "few," "soon" aren't helpful. They are subject to interpretation. "Tuesday," "50%," "seventeen" are clear. You and others can know for certain if you are progressing, maintaining, or regressing.

QUIZ yourself as well as others about progress. Ask questions. Why are we doing this? Who else should be involved? Is this the best way? Why do we think this will work? Here's a hint. Write down those questions. When you write them, they won't go away. You'll have to answer them. Then write down your answers! This is a great discipline. Try it!

RATE yourself and, by all means, be honest! Are you doing what really needs to be done? Are you doing it as well as you can? How do you know? This is always difficult for all of us because we don't like to acknowledge our own faults. But if we don't measure, we'll never know where we are, could be, or should be.

REACH out and look for new options and new possibilities. Also, reach out for new people and the chance to put them into new positions. As a manager, you can influence what happens around you, to you, and to others. Don't wait for things "to happen." Make them happen!

READ not only the typical material, like papers and newsletters. Read people, conditions, and options. All too often we get caught up in routine activities, and we miss possibilities right in front of us. Many of us *look*, but we don't *see*. And then we miss great opportunities.

REALIZE that you can influence what happens around you. Regardless of your job, you constantly relate to other people in all walks of life. You can be an equal player if you first recognize and then use all the talents you have. You can change the future if you work at it!

REBOUND fast after adversity because the rest of the world is constantly moving and changing. The longer you wait, the more you have to do just to catch up to where you were before the adversity. Determine first what went wrong, then why it went wrong, and then how you can change the conditions. Then change them!

RECALL what worked for you in the past – and what didn't. Then determine how you can manage those conditions. Certainly you must focus on future events, but a focused look and honest reflection on the past will help you make the right decisions in the future and avoid the pitfalls of the past. Everybody makes mistakes, but don't make the same mistakes twice.

RECOMMEND the actions you believe in. Don't wait for others to figure out what you already know. Then, where appropriate, identify and recommend the people who can carry out those actions. Delegate. Don't try to do everything yourself. First of all, you can't do everything, and second, you shouldn't use all your energy that way. Help others to help you.

RECRUIT others with talent and then teach them how to grow and apply those talents. Keep looking ahead, identifying opportunities, and matching people to those tasks. They'll be grateful for the assistance, and you'll benefit knowing you helped someone to grow. In the future, that someone might be in a position to help you, too.

REDUCE the unnecessary pressures you put on yourself and the pressures others feel too. All too often we set goals that are unrealistic, then we become frustrated, and we give up. Lofty goals are important, but remember to recognize the intermediate steps that must be taken to reach a summit. Go for the summit, bur concentrate on one step at a time.

REFER to past events and current conditions when you plan future activities. Knowing the past will help you navigate. Read signs just as you would use a road map on a car trip. Only foolish people "go it alone" without using maps and charts. Life is too important to ad lib!

REFINE your actions and activities. In most situations, a new idea has some rough edges that need to be smoothed out. Do this "smoothing" before you begin. Your focus will be better, and your actions will be more productive. Reduce friction for better progress.

REFLECT on where you are using your talent and your energy. Take some quiet time and do an honest, internal evaluation. For most of us, it's difficult to see ourselves as others see us, but since we obviously know ourselves far better than anyone else does, we must be honest with what we see. Determine the what, why, and how of your life and your expectations.

REFRESH yourself and your outlook by getting away from your daily routine. No matter the job you have, step away once in a while and recharge your batteries. Things always look different from a distance so step away and develop a new perspective and a new outlook.

REHEARSE activities whenever you can. It's unusual for any behavior to be perfect on the first try, so when you have only one chance to perform, don't risk the success. Rehearse it. Make the mistakes in the rehearsal, fix them, and then perform. When you give a sales presentation, for example, you want to create a good image or you'll lose the sale. When you apply for a new position, you want to create that positive image. After all, you're selling yourself. Rehearse what you want to say and how you want to say it. Because you'll get only one shot, make it count!

RELAX whenever you can. Nobody can continue to work without taking a break. If you try to do that, you'll soon lose productivity; your standards will diminish; and you'll waste time, talent, and energy. You'll find that as soon as you return from that break, you'll perform better, and the "lost time" will be more than made up.

REMAIN consistent. It's difficult for everyone to face the challenges that arise every day, and many buckle under the pressure or give in. If you stay true to your core values, decisions are easy regardless of the pressures you face. Every decision ultimately comes down to a simple yes/no choice. Consistency and staying true to your core values will help you make that choice every time.

REMEMBER those around you who contributed to helping you get to where you are now. Every one of us has benefited – or suffered – because of the actions of others. Be aware of what others have done for you and look for ways to repay those contributions. This isn't simply "repaying a debt," it's the right thing to do!

REMIND yourself of all you have, and then use it wisely. When you get caught up in problems and conflicts, the world around you can seem overpowering. Take some time and step back to see exactly what you have. Don't focus only on what you don't have. Build on a positive base, and the results will continue to be positive.

REMOVE obstacles. Get them out of your way, but use good sense. If you can't remove them or go through them, go around them. Find another route. When you have a destination, keep moving toward it. A detour on a road trip is an annoyance, but when you have a destination, you deal with that annoyance and get where you want to go.

REPORT to yourself! So many times we focus only on reporting to others. That reporting is good and necessary, but remember this: You're the one who knows your intentions best, so "check up" on yourself every once in a while. Give yourself a "Report Card" on how you're doing. You'll be surprised – hopefully pleased – and certainly enlightened.

REQUIRE of yourself what you require of others. This is a "spin" on the Golden Rule. Take a moment sometime and write down a list of the traits and qualities you expect and admire in others. Then ask yourself if you demonstrate those same traits and qualities. If so – good for you! If not – why not?

RESIGN yourself to the fact you're not perfect, that you don't always do your best, that you can improve your behavior. Then set about making the necessary adjustments. Change what you can, but live with what you can't. Find alternatives!

RESOLVE the problems and the behaviors that get in the way of working well with those around you. Colleague, customer, family pressures develop every day, but support and assistance can also be found in these same people if you look for and encourage it. If you start the resolution process, others will follow.

RESPECT your colleagues and your customers. Even when you're sure they "just don't get it," try again to be of assistance. Respect demands action from you. Listen and observe, then process what you learn. That just might open up new opportunities for you.

RESTRICT your activities to the things that will help you grow in your job. The business world is full of distractions and detours, but they'll give you trouble only if you let them. Be in charge of your opportunities, and take the initiative.

REWARD yourself for a job well done. All too often people focus on their shortcomings. It's important to recognize them, of course, but allow yourself to be pleased, too. When you get in the habit of rewarding yourself (when it's well deserved) – and others, too – you'll be surprised at how well your days progress.

REVIEW what you have done when you come to end of your every day. What worked, and what didn't? Why? Many people get caught up in the "big picture" and forget that it's made up of many tiny brush strokes. Your end-of-the-day reality check will help you see all the brush strokes.

REVISE plans and activities when you see they aren't taking you where you want to go. It has been said often that only a fool will continue to do something the same way over and over again and hope for a different outcome. Don't be a fool!

RISK trying something new. When you were very young, you took risks all the time, and you never saw them as something to be avoided. Think of the child learning to walk. There was a big risk with every step! Learning to talk was a big risk too, because the child might mispronounce a word. But the child risked – and the child grew. Do the same thing as an adult. Take a risk!

ROCK the boat from time to time. It's one way to check your stability and the stability of your department, as well as your own talents. A little practice rocking the boat while in calm waters can help you learn how to handle the rough seas when they come at you.

RUN your life and your business from minute to minute. Be in charge at all times because you can't know how much time you have. If you wait for things to "just happen," you'll probably miss opportunities. Take care of the minutes, and the present, the days, and the future will be on strong footing.

RUSH in to provide assistance to customers and support to colleagues. All too often managers watch and then criticize rather than teach and encourage. Look for opportunities to help. Your actions will be appreciated and returned in kind. We often hear a lot about "building relationships." This is how you do it!

SAIL along, taking advantage of the "winds of change" that surround you. That doesn't mean simply moving whichever way the wind is blowing. That can lead to confusion and loss of direction. Any good sailor knows that he can sail *into* the wind just as he can sail *with* it. Certainly, that takes skill, but that's what's expected of a good manager – as well as a good parent.

SATISFY your own curiosity and the curiosity of others. That means taking chances where appropriate. Most people are comfortable doing things they know well. Doing something new is frightening. But it's also exciting! And you just might open up new vistas you never knew existed for you. Take a chance!

SAVOR successes and gains, but don't stop there. When defeats or failures show themselves to you, savor them, too, because they'll help you grow in new directions. Everything in life doesn't come easily or smoothly. But rough surfaces, when properly applied, can smooth and buff other surfaces. Just ask a cabinetmaker about the benefits of sandpaper.

SCAN your entire environment, and then stop to focus on the specific parts of it. Don't just *look* at your surroundings. *See* them. *Focus* on them. *Think* about them. Explore all the dimensions at your disposal. Look at, around, and under. Your change of perspective might provide exciting – and surprising – results.

SELL ideas and concepts. Sell yourself. No one in the world knows as much about you as you do so help the world know all about you. Don't wait for other people to ask questions. Volunteer information. Others might not even know what questions to ask you, but you know what is important for them to know. Take the initiative!

SEIZE opportunities – and seize challenges, too. They are the two sides of the same coin, and they are affected by your point of view. When you have direction and focus, you can adapt to changing conditions. When you can adapt while others only react, you'll make progress. Those others will fall behind!

SEQUENCE your action. Determine what has to be done and figure out the most appropriate order of action. All too often activity takes the place of accomplishment because the players don't plan ahead. It's tempting to "do something – anything," but that's usually a costly decision. Remember that old adage: "Haste makes waste."

SERVE first. Accept later. If and when you help others by offering whatever services you can, you improve the lives of those others. You also, at the same time, improve your own life. You don't serve others just to get something in return, but you will always reap the benefits of your service to others.

SET goals. Set timetables. Set limits. Make plans so you can control your activities and the impact you have on others. If you flounder and drift, you'll be moving but without direction. You'll miss opportunities and advantages. Set a course and follow it to where you want to go. You can always change course, of course, but that will be a conscious decision. Take control!

SETTLE into a routine because that can lead to stability, but stay alert to new opportunities as they present themselves, and seek out those new activities. Stability doesn't mean complacency! If you settle in – and stay in – a "groove" for a long time, it can become a "rut." That usually becomes boring and you can lose enthusiasm and creativity.

SHARE what you know with both superiors and subordinates. As a manager, one of your primary responsibilities is to be a teacher. Teach your staff what they need to know to be successful. Then inform your superiors. Keep them in the loop, not to ask permission for every step you take, but to keep the communication lines open in all directions.

SHOW that you're interested. And that showing must be clear to your staff and to those to whom you report. Talk is cheap, but action speaks volumes. Demonstrate your interest, your concern, your ability, and your focus. What you don't know about, ask. Help others show what they know. Teach them "the ropes."

SIT tight until you know where to go. Planning a clear course of action will assure that, once you begin to move, you'll be moving in the right direction. A little well placed and timed hesitation will provide a greater possibility of success.

SMILE because that will make others smile, too. Many of us get so wrapped up in our own thoughts and activities that we forget how we appear to those around us. Set a positive tone by being positive. A pleasant appearance can work wonders in setting that tone.

SOLVE problems by using all the tools at your disposal. Those "tools," of course, include the people with whom you are in constant contact every day. They have ideas, preferences, expectations, and experiences different from yours. Gather that information, and put it to work.

SPECIFY what you want and need. Don't expect others around you to "figure out" what you mean and want. They can't get inside your head and, through some magic process, understand you. It's your job to inform them if you expect cooperation or positive reactions from them. So be specific, and tell them exactly what you want.

SPIN isn't a bad four-letter word just because we hear it used so often in reference to political events. It refers to putting events into a context relevant to specific situations. When you explain activities and situations to others in order to help them understand a business or a family decision, it's a "spin." It's your perception, and you're entitled to it.

STABILIZE rocky situations and relationships by first gathering the data necessary to understand a situation. If you react to what seems to be a problem situation you might over react and cause greater problems. Like setting a course, you must maintain balance and avoid sudden moves or you could be in deep trouble!

STANDARDIZE whenever possible, but don't stifle creativity. Using common elements and processes can be profitable, but be sure to be on the lookout for possible improvements. Don't stop progress for the sake of preserving current activities. You could easily lose momentum and market advantage.

STEER a course by using a reference point and a good compass. To do that successfully requires that you know two things: where you are and where you want to go. Without both of those, movement will be random and accidental. When you have both points in mind, it's easy to plot a course.

STIMULATE both ideas and the people around you who have them. And you can do both simultaneously. If you start by including those others in decision making, you'll discover quickly how those new ideas will flow – sometimes reinforcing yours and sometimes challenging them. But always invigorating them!

STOP doing what doesn't work. When you discover that certain activities don't produce the results you expect, explore other options. You can't expect results to change if you repeat the same behaviors. You'll just waste time. And there's no percentage in doing that.

STRETCH out of your comfort zone from time to time. Look for new ways and new opportunities. Most of us get very comfortable repeating behaviors because they feel good. But on the job and at home, our challenge and our mission shouldn't be to just feel good. It should be to be good. Try something new. See what happens.

STRUGGLE to overcome the feelings of uncertainty that inhibit or slow down activity. It's always tempting to do the same things over and over, and that can lead to developing strong habits. If the habits are productive and positive, that might be a good thing. But don't simply assume that "comfortable" is the most productive. Experiment with new approaches.

SUGGEST modifications rather than demand changes. Being gentle, especially at the start of an association can help build positive relationships. "Coming on too strong" is usually met with resistance. Then any progress is very difficult. Take it easy at first. Save the "force" for later if you need it.

SUMMARIZE what you have accomplished at the end of every day. Fill out a mental report card on how you used the time available to you every day. You'll probably discover something very interesting. When you do those evaluations (and no one but you knows about them), you'll see how much you have accomplished – and you'll see clearly what still needs to be done. Then you have tomorrow to do it!

TAKE ADVANTAGE of opportunities but not of people. Seeing possibilities in situations and events is sound practice in business and, in family life, and that results in growth and development. Seeing and acting on the weaknesses of others is exploitation and demeaning. Others will remember both types of behaviors. It's up to you to decide which legacy you want.

TALK to the people around you, family, and associates. Then listen to what they have to say, but really *listen*! Pay attention. Then ask questions or offer comments when you talk again. This dialogue will produce a positive atmosphere, one in which you can solve problems and explore opportunities.

THANK others for their service and advice. A well-placed "thank you" goes a long way in strengthening relationships and encouraging others to seek better and better levels of performance. Don't just thank those to whom you report. Thank those who report to you! An old adage tells us this: "If someone is nice to you in a restaurant but isn't nice to the waiter, don't trust him. He isn't a nice person. Good advice!

THINK first, then talk. Sounds obvious, but all too often people do just the opposite. They say the first thing that comes to them, then they have to rethink the response and apologize for the reaction they caused. You'll have fewer occasions in which to apologize if you talk only after thinking about a situation. What's your hurry anyway?

TOLERATE conditions when you have no other choices, but change those unpleasant conditions when – and as soon as – you can. This doesn't mean you have to accept, and later endure, a poor situation. It means you must recognize the relevant events, then explain it, determine why that situation exists, then use the resources available to you to change the conditions. But take that action slowly and deliberately.

TRADE the "comfortable" for the "challenging." Reach out and explore. It's okay to take acceptable risks. In fact, when you take those, you'll see more clearly what you can accomplish. Without risk there is complacency, and the next stop is usually boredom. That's not a good neighborhood to live in.

TRAVEL to places you haven't visited already. Those places don't have to be far away. They could be at the other end of the building where you work, a different floor, or a different department. Go for a visit. Check with your boss or HR to get ideas and introductions. You'll be surprised what you can encounter if only you ask, look, and move out of your comfort zone. There's a big world out there. Take a look at it!

TRIGGER new ideas by challenging what you think you already know well. Look for ways to combine two or three separate ideas into something new. Once you start this process, your world will become more exciting because you'll look at things through new eyes. When you share what you see with others, they might try it, too. That could lead to many and varied new insights.

TRUST your colleagues and your subordinates to do what is right. You don't have a monopoly on accuracy and brilliance. Give others a chance and observe what happens. Usually, they will grow, develop, and produce. If they don't, perhaps your role must change to that of a teacher. Teach the others how to grow, develop, and produce.

TRY something new when the "old way" seems to become less and less productive. Times change, conditions change, and people change. If you persist in doing things the same way over and over again, the changing scene will probably pass you by. Don't wait until you are forced to change just to "catch up." It might be too late. Try a new option today.

USE what you have. Everyone is different with different talents and abilities. Identify the unique characteristics that make you interesting and "one of a kind." Then hone and develop them in order to become comfortable in your own personality. You aren't, can't be, and never will be anyone else. So use what you have to make you a strong individual.

UNRAVEL situations that are complicated for your staff. Your experience and perceptions give you a different perspective from theirs. Help them navigate through the complexities of the situations that are new and complicated to them. Again, become a good teacher!

VALIDATE your ideas. Check data, and question why you feel the way you do about situations. Challenge yourself. And challenge others too. Don't argue or find fault. Use discovery and observation. Then modify wherever necessary.

VALUE the time, the talents, and the desires of those with whom you come in contact every day. They are all part of your life and your experiences, so take advantage of what they can offer to you. You can't "go it alone" all the time, so develop and foster relationships that can be helpful for you and for them, too.

VARY your activities and your behaviors. When things are working well and as expected, keep going, but look for ways to work smarter. The very best way to do almost anything hasn't been found yet, so keep looking – and keep trying. You can always go back to the old way if necessary.

VIEW conditions from the perspective of others. You know what you want and prefer, but others might have contrasting – or complementary – wants and needs. Take time to consider the viewpoints of others as you make your decisions. Multiple perspectives can assure an accurate course of action.

VISIT new worlds. You don't have to travel thousands of miles to do that. All you have to do is to expend your current activities. If you haven't visited a new museum near your home, go to it. Read a book you heard about but never took time to read. Go to a library (rather than the internet) and check out a book you never heard about. Read it, and see where it leads you!

VISUALIZE what "might be" and what "could be." Break out of the comfortable old habits once in a while to look at the world a little differently. Let your imagination go to work. Be a child again and "make believe." Look at clouds and see what wonders you can find in them. Be creative – on the job and at home.

VOLUNTEER to do what needs to be done. Take on the tasks others don't want to assume. There will be two results. First, the job will get done, and second, others will see your contribution. Growth, development, and advancement in business are determined by individual performance and the observations of others. Be in the forefront even when the tasks are menial, and the pleasant ones will come your way with frequency and abundance.

VOTE with your actions, not just with your words. Stand up and be counted. Even though that might feel uncomfortable at first, you'll be pleasantly surprised at what you can gain from a firm base on a solid foundation. Clarify that base by staking out and demonstrating a consistent position.

WAIT until you're ready and until conditions are right before you undertake a project. If you jump to conclusions and leap into action too quickly, you might move in the wrong direction. An old adage tells us to: "Make haste slowly." Great advice. First, look. Then evaluate.

Finally, act. You'll be more productive, and you'll be on safer ground!

WAKE UP to the possibilities all around you. Only you will be able to do that because only you know what your world includes. Only you know what you want to do – what you want to accomplish. Go for it! Force yourself out of the complacency that comes from repetition and look for the new, the exciting, the stimulating. Move out!

WIN the respect of others through what you do, but don't expect to get it just because you demand it. By demanding, you might get obedience, but that's a long way from respect, support, and allegiance. Obedience might be fine for the short term, but respect will serve you well in the long run. The first, obedience, is immediate and temporary, but the second, respect, is important and durable

WING it, and you might succeed, but more often you'll either fail or "just get by." Nothing can take the place of preparation and planning. After completing those, be sure to rehearse. How others perceive us is determined by what they see us do and by what we say, so be careful. Certainly, you don't have to calculate every action. That could lead to hypocrisy, but be aware of how your behavior is judged by others and act accordingly.

WONDER what might be next, what might come your way, what you might be able to accomplish if you open your mind to new possibilities. Allow yourself to look at the world with a new set of eyes. Don't just see things as they are, see them as they might be. When you look for new horizons, you'll find them.

WORK to achieve a goal, don't just hope it will come to you. It's important to have hopes and dreams, but they are abstract, and you can't control them or get your arms around them. Work, on the other hand, speaks to direction, movement, and behavior. You can control your behavior, so work on it, and you'll see the progress you can make.

YIELD when necessary, but be sure it is indeed necessary. Stand your ground when your core values tell you that's the right thing to do. A firm set of standards will make life much easier and much more productive on the job and with your family. Most things are easy to do when you "want" to do them. Ask yourself this simple question: "What do I want to do?" Now do it!

END PAGE

A Final Thought

Well, you've made it through all three hundred items. I hope you found them enjoyable and valuable. I hope you picked up a few ideas along the way, and, most of all, I hope you'll be able to use some of them as you continue working with colleagues, family, and customers. Finally, I hope we can visit again. I would like to hear from you.

Please feel free to e-mail me at:

joropa@northwestern.edu

or visit my web site at: www.jrparkinson.com,

About the Author

Bob Parkinson has served as a communications consult-ant and coach for numerous Fortune 500 companies working successfully at all levels of corporate, govern-ment, and academic institutions from CEO's to new hires. In addition, he has taught more than 1750 com-munication related programs for clients in the U.S. and internationally and consulted and conducted research in South America, Africa, and Australia.

He earned a Ph.D. degree from Syracuse University. His other degrees are: MA in Management and Supervi-sion, and BA in English and Biology from Montclair State University (NJ).

After serving on active duty in the U.S. Army, Parkin-son began his professional career as a high school teacher. Subsequent professional positions include: Faculty, Northwestern University; Associate Dean, Na-tional Louis University; Director of Research, Office of the Governor, IL; Director of Research, Bell & Howell. He lives with his wife, Eileen, in Sarasota, Florida.